The Product

Written By:

Marcus A. Parker

authorHOUSE

1663 Liberty Drive, Suite 200
Bloomington, Indiana 47403
(800) 839-8640
www.authorhouse.com

First published by AuthorHouse 07/08/04

ISBN: 1-4184-6258-6 (e)
ISBN: 1-4184-6257-8 (sc)

Library of Congress Control Number: 2004094185

Printed in the United States of America
Bloomington, Indiana

This book is printed on acid-free paper.

"An individual has not started living until he can rise above the narrow confines of his individualistic concerns to the broader concerns of all humanity."
Rev. Dr. Martin Luther King Jr.

"Success is measured not so much by the position one has reached in life as by the obstacles one has overcome while trying to succeed."
Booker T Washington

This book is dedicated to the memory of my grandfather, the late Ora Mitchell Sr. **(Mitch)**

"No matter what accomplishments you make, somebody helps you."

Wilma Rudolph

Table of Contents

"The only justification for ever looking down on somebody is to pick them up"
Rev. Jesse Jackson

About the Author

Marcus Parker was born in Port Arthur, Tx in 1974. He grew up during the rise of the crack cocaine epidemic and witnessed many people fall victim to the disease. Despite his humble beginnings, surrounded by negativity, he became financially independent and walked away from a six-figure income at the age of twenty-seven. Having accomplished so much in such a short period of time, Marcus revisits his past to find the root of his drive and motivation. The Product, highlights the events, let downs, and victories that he faced on this journey. Marcus' dream is to encourage others by sharing his story and the values that propelled him along the way. Parker credits all of his success to his family, a strong community, and most of all, faith in God.

"How far you go in life depends on your being tender with the young, compassionate with the aged, sympathetic with the striving, and tolerant of the weak and strong. Because some day in life you will have been all these."

George Washington Carver

Acknowledgements

First I would like to thank God for giving me the strength to press on from day to day. I would also like to thank all of my family and friends in Port Arthur, TX. Thank-you for staying in my corner and always supporting me in every way. I would like to thank my wife, Rolanda and children, Sydney and Marcus Jr. You all are the reason I try so hard. I would like to thank my father for always trying his absolute best. This book is also a dream come true for my mother, who always encouraged me to write down the events of my life every step of the way. I also pray that my children can read this and realize just how much their father loves them and to learn that no obstacles can stand in your way as long as you put God first in your life and stay focused on your goals.

"Hold fast to dreams, for if dreams die, life is a broken winged bird that cannot fly."
Langston Hughes

Introduction

This book takes you on a journey of a young man constantly battling negativity and insecurity, but determined to change his financial destiny for himself and his family.

This book was not written to teach individuals how to make money. It was written to highlight something much more important. It was written to show that anything is possible in life regardless of who you are, if you are diligent and stay focused on your true goals. Success in life can come in many forms. Whatever level of success you are looking to achieve can be attained using the values pointed out in this book along with faith in God. My wish is that you can walk with me throughout my life and get an understanding of how adversity in your life can be used as the fuel to drive you in a positive direction. I truly feel that God has given me a gift to share with others. I hope that

Marcus A. Parker

this book can help you grow and find your own
level of success in life.

"Education is our passport to the future, for tomorrow belongs to the people who prepare for it today."
Malcolm X

Statistics

-Black families have the highest percentage of families in the United States living at or below the poverty level.

-Single women head 69% of all black households

-60% of all children in the black community are fatherless and without a black role model in the home.

-One out of four black men are in jail or on parole.

-60% of all black males are in prisons, the other half into drug and alcohol abuse or unemployed, unskilled, or high school dropouts.

- State prisons contain more than 5 % of all black males in their 20s.

These and many more statistics can be found by researching the Bureau of Justice Statistics and well as the US census bureau. You can also search the internet to get statistics from other sources such as city or county info or university research. These facts can be quite alarming when we realize that these are not just numbers on paper. They are our mothers, fathers, uncles, nephews, cousins etc. These figures represent real human life. They represent us, and people we love. Even though I've heard these facts all my life, I had no idea that some of the numbers actually increased in the southern region of the United States. Statistics like these tend to raise the ever-so popular question; Are we, as young black people really <u>The Product</u> of our surroundings?

This is where my story begins:

"A dream doesn't become reality through magic; it takes sweat, determination and hard work."
Colin Powell

The Product

Statistically, in America
It's hard to be young and black
With so many of us locked away in jail
And so many strung out on crack

So many of us in poverty
Negativity on our minds
Battling unemployment
And contemplating crimes

High blood pressure and Diabetes
Our lives always at stake
Disgusted with our situations
Running from our fate

Uneducated, since we weren't
Ever taught to get ahead
Just trying to live better than our peers
Who are locked away or dead

Always accustomed to negativity
Yet wishing for the day
That someone could come around us
With positive things to say

Marcus A. Parker

My life just seems so limited
As I look around I see
A handful of successful folks
But none that look like me

But there is hope, we will survive
Living better than before
We'll learn to accept positivity
But negativity, we'll ignore

We will learn to respect our elders
For they truly paid the price
For us to have the freedom
To live a better life

We will regain our sense of pride
In ourselves as well as our seed
And learn to put our faith in God
The formula to succeed

We will continue to persevere
To get where we belong
We're <u>THE PRODUCT</u> of years of adversity
But it only made us strong

Marcus A. Parker

"I don't know the key to success, but the key to failure is trying to please everybody."
Bill Cosby

Autobiography

I was born in a small town in Texas called Port Arthur in 1974. I was the only child of Richard Allen and Martha Parker. As a child I spent lots of time to myself to think and reflect on life and the things around me. The city I grew up in had little industry outside of refinery work, which at the time was slowly going downward. There was a large degree of poverty and drugs in the area. This was the beginning of the crack cocaine epidemic and I watched many people around me fall victim to the disease. My parents did a great job of working with what we were given. My father worked as a sewage plant operator for the city earning approx. 17 thousand per year. My mother stayed at home and watched children for friends to earn extra income.

I learned very early on that hard work would make me successful. I found hard work to be my escape. That was the arena where I felt complete peace. I literally spent hours thinking about what it would take for us to become wealthy. For the life of me, I couldn't figure out how people could financially live the lives that I had seen on television. There were families with nice homes and multiple vehicles. They would vacation and do lots of activities. These families always seemed to have a really positive attitude about everything. This lifestyle seemed so impossible based on my family's financial struggles. We were always trying to stay afloat. Ironically, I would often hear local folks say how good we had it, and that we were lucky because my father had such a good job. I couldn't understand that if my father had such a good job, why were we always broke, why were we always struggling, why was there such a high degree of negativity in the air? This question would spin through my head millions of times as a child.

Although I had never seen or met a wealthy person, somehow I always felt that I would become wealthy. I would dream of being a scientist or an inventor. I was very good with electronics and would often take old toys off of trash piles and open them to take out the batteries, motors, lights etc. I would spend hours and hours in my room tinkering with my findings until I created something worth showing off to my family. Often the inventions would be some sort of robot whose body consisted of a small cardboard box. My cardboard creation would often be able to move forward and back with the remote control taken from one of those old remote control cars with a wire between the remote and the car. The eyes would usually light up and the arms would spin. As a result of these events, I was soon labeled "smart", by my family. Smart was not the coolest thing to be through the eyes of the neighborhood kids, so I rarely took my creations outside of the house. This was a label that I didn't need at the time. I was teased enough by my peers about my parents.

My father was an alcoholic and my mother was an albino(meaning that she had the appearance of a white person). Growing up in an all black neighborhood, kids would often say that I was adopted and that my mother was white. I was teased a lot about this. They were also full of stories about seeing my father drunk, sleeping in the car, or driving off the road. Etc. My father was committed into an Alcoholic's Anonymous program on four different occasions throughout my childhood for an average of 30 to 60 days each time.

I had to take speech classes at school to help me correct a lisp in my speech. Basicly, I couldn't say the "S" sound without sticking out my tongue.

For some reason, I always felt like I didn't quite fit in with everyone around me. My self-esteem was very low and I always thought very little of myself. I rarely ever gave my parents any trouble. I would often wonder why things seemed so wrong for me when I knew that I was such a good person.

I spent lots of time in church as a child. I had a very close relationship with God, and I would often pray many times throughout the day. I accepted Jesus Christ as my Lord and Savior at a very young age. My mother made me read my bible pretty often and people would always tell me that I would be a preacher one day.

In the mid-eighties, I learned how to swim at a city pool a block or so from our house. This pool was near an area of town that has since become known as "the Cutz or Short Texas." This is where you could find the drugs. This area always had heavy traffic back in those days. From the pool you could watch people selling and smoking crack on a daily basis. Everyone in the city knew that if you had a friend or family member who sold or smoked dope, you could always find him or her near this area. It was also not rare to witness a fight, or to see people get shot or stabbed. Back in those days, shooting and stabbing didn't happen near as often as fist-fights, but I've witnessed my share. My mother was very protective, so I knew that if I told her what went on over there, she would have prevented me from going back. Me and the other kids that were good swimmers would often get to help clean out the debris that the dope fiends would usually throw in the pool during the night. We would retrieve mostly empty wine bottles and beer caps.

My mother was the oldest of nine children. She had seven brothers and a younger sister. My uncles were always more like older brothers to me. They taught me everything they knew about life. Most of them had their share of legal issues and we watched drugs and prison rip my family apart. As I watched my uncles struggle with these issues as well as unemployment, I realized that if I were going to be a success in life that I would have to stay out of trouble with the law. I also watched how that first criminal record put them in a category that made them virtually unemployable, especially being in an area where jobs were very limited. All of them had their own strong points but one thing they all did well was play table tennis or ping pong. I would love to stay over at my grandmother's house so that I could play ping pong with them. Everywhere that I traveled later on in life, I was able to beat just about anyone in ping pong.

When I was about nine, my older cousin Doug was murdered on the morning of his sixteenth birthday. He was about six years older than me so, needless to say, I looked up to him. I remembered going to his football games and eating with him at our grandparent's house, and now he was gone. I found myself paranoid of turning sixteen from that point on.

My parents would fight a lot and I often found myself in the middle of the arguments. I would try my best to be somewhat of a mediator and try to bring peace to the household. I remember vividly, counseling my father so he could say the right things to make my mother happy. Whenever someone in the house was down or depressed, it would make me feel down as well. I somehow always felt ultimately responsible for keeping the peace even though I rarely ever gave my parents any trouble at all.

I made all A's as an elementary student and was moved into an advanced program called "summit" for my efforts. Somehow I always felt that if I could make my parents proud they wouldn't have to fight anymore.

I started in the summit program in the third grade. This was my first time going to class with kids of different races. This experience taught me lots of things. I never had to feel ashamed or guilty about being called "smart" anymore.

I also found that compared to a lot of the other kids, I wasn't as smart as I thought I was. I learned right away that most of the kids in my class did not have the financial difficulties that I had at home. This advanced program often called for additional school supplies that were always a strain for us to buy. The kids in my class really liked me. I think it had a lot to do with the fact that I was the class clown. I think comedy always kept me from focusing in on all the grown up things that I worried about at home. One of my white friends would give me a quarter everyday during lunch so I could have an ice cream with him. I knew that my mother would have objected to me taking money from him so I never told her until now. If you can remember being nine or ten years old, it was very hard to pass up desert back then. I figured that I owe him about 30 dollars, and I plan on giving it to him whenever I see him again. The class would often go on fieldtrips to places like museums, exhibits and educational plays. I got a chance visit places that I never would have gotten an opportunity to see. Some of my classmate's parents were professionals like doctors and lawyers. I noticed that these kids concentrated on being kids and never thought about money matters. Money or the lack thereof was all I thought about. Everyday I would dread the moment that the class would be asked for something that my family couldn't afford.

As far back as I can remember, I had some sort of business working. I was really good at origami(the art of folding paper), so I would make little things like airplanes, animals, etc. with paper and sell them to the other kids for pocket change. At home, I would make little bookstands out of wood and also made plaques out of plaster and sold them to friends, relatives and neighbors. Once I set up a lemonade stand along with the rest of my inventory in front of my house. For a while, I would get a check in the mail every month for cutting grass at a neighbor's house. I also had my mother's bathroom up and running as a barbershop when I got to high school. This started with a pair of clippers from the store that I bought to cut my hair. Before I knew it, people were lined up at my house for a haircut. I charged two dollars per haircut and I would make approximately an extra 40 dollars per week. With all of the ventures I was working, the goal was to save one thousand dollars. I never did reach this goal but I gave it my all.

After years of fighting and disagreements, my parents finally divorced when I was around 14 years old. Just prior to this, my father was fired from his job with the city for being intoxicated on duty, and we were flat broke. For years there were never any additional funds, but now there were no funds at all. I can still remember like yesterday, when my father's co-worker brought over his last paycheck. His final two-week check came out to about 60 dollars, so the other co-workers had all chipped in to give my mother a helping hand to pay our bills. I watched as she cried for hours about our situation as well as the extreme generosity of my father's co-workers.

At this point, my life was changed forever. Not only was I the man of the house, but also now an adult. This event, like most others in the past, showed me that it was the lack of money that brought tears, pain, hurt, and misery to the family. From that point on, everything that I did had to be related to making money, making progress, or both.

Shortly after my father was fired, he and my mother received their share of his retirement money. This small lump sum lasted about a year, and it was back to the drawing board. My father was nice enough to buy me a car with a portion of his funds. The vehicle was a 1977 Chevy Nova. The car cost 700 dollars, and my father made me promise that I would take care of everything such as gas maintenance and insurance. I agreed and was on my way. I was 15 at the time and was able to get a hardship driver's license because my mother was legally blind. I was very happy to have a vehicle and also very appreciative. I made sure that the car insurance was paid every month. I had always had an interest in car stereos and amplifiers, so I immediately started to install music in my car with the money from my job. As with all of my ventures, I was teased for trying to create a sound system with limited funds. Soon I got extremely good at it and others wanted me to install their sound system. I made money doing this, but if money was not available, I would instead take collateral such as radios, amplifiers, speakers, or equalizers as a payment. I would also sell these things to other people. If I had some equipment that I needed to sell, I would install it in my car and ride around

Marcus A. Parker

with it until someone offered to buy it. This never took very long because I had developed a reputation and I would install the equipment for free if they bought it from me. In addition to the entrepreneurial ventures I also worked for the local newspaper, a grocery store, and a sandwich shop.

The last job I worked before turning 18 really changed my life completely. I worked with a summer program called PHS (Program for Human Services). This program allowed kids of low-income households to have the ability to work in professional settings. We worked in various departments for the city for most of the summer. I worked in the Personnel department of city hall. I spent this summer working side by side with true professionals. I realized several valuable lessons during my time there. The first thing I realized was that these professionals were ordinary people. They worked jobs that many people had the ability to do, but they also had the qualifications. It was like a light went off in my head telling me that this wonderful group of individuals were able to reap the benefits of gainful employment by making themselves qualified to do so. That summer I did all types of administrative work such as answering the telephone, making copies, faxing and filing. The people I worked with were the friendliest people I had ever met and I loved them. They had lots of admiration for me based on my character, and for having an additional job at the time. They would constantly tell me what a great young man I was, and what a great job my mother did in raising such a responsible, industrious young man.

I can remember them asking if I made straight A's in school. This was actually an embarrassing moment for me because I didn't make straight A's. Although I had always been in advanced classes, I rarely cared about grades anymore. I remember making all A's and B's up until I was about in the seventh grade. This is when I realized that an A or a B wasn't going to change my life in any form or fashion.(At least that's what I thought.) I had been thinking that making money was much more important than making good grades. I learned that summer that I couldn't have been more wrong. Those grades meant everything. In the personnel department we would receive lots of applications for jobs, and I watched how important it was for a person to look good on paper. Some applications came in nice and neat and others would come in folded right out of a persons back pocket. I vowed never to sell myself short on paper again as I had done with my grades.

This experience really set the tone for things to come in my life. I always did whatever I could to look good on paper and qualify myself for anything I wanted to do in life. At the end of that summer PHS had an awards ceremony where I was crowned King of the program for that summer. After that, I went back to school for my senior year and averaged all A's and B's.

While still a senior in high school, I was making grown up decisions for myself and my mother, who at this time, was divorced. After many painful repairs to keep the Nova running, I decided to do something about it. One day, while sitting in English class, I found a 1980 Honda Accord for sale in the paper located about 20 miles away. Immediately after school I jumped in the car and started my mission.

When I arrived in the Nova, which was back-firing at the time, the salesman told me that he didn't want the car but he admired the fact that a school-aged kid drove all that way to buy his car. When it was time to test-drive the Honda, I noticed that it was a five-speed manual transmission. I was never taught to drive a stick shift so I had the salesman test drive it for me while I watched him. I bought it that day even though I didn't know how to drive it. I drove home with the car stopping every time I came to a stop sign. That day I taught myself how to drive a stick shift. Two weeks later, the transmission died in the vehicle. I took it to a local transmission shop, who quoted the price to fix it at 400 dollars. I only had three hundred dollars, so I gave it to the owner who agreed to fix it and wait for me to bring back the last hundred. I went back the next week and paid him. He also told me that I had good credit with him and he would help me anytime in the future.

My mother and I probably had one of the closest relationships that a young man can have with his mother. We always talked about anything. We would walk to church together and we were even Baptized on the same day. Even when my mother had to whip me, it was almost like we both had an understanding that she was just doing what she had to do. I always considered us very close friends.

When I was seventeen, my mother decided to have a talk with me. She sat me down and told me that my father I had known all my life was not my biological father. She also went on to tell me that my biological father was a man that I had known for years. Words cannot explain how much this absolutely crushed me. I realized that I wasn't exactly the person who I thought I was. I was really hurt even more when I thought about all of the years of my life feeling like I didn't fit in and to now know the reason. Since I never could explain this empty feeling, I never told anyone. The irony was that for years, kids would tell me that I was adopted because my mother looked Caucasian. Now the truth was out. I was also very resentful towards my biological father since I knew that his family didn't have the financial difficulty that my mother and I had. When my mother and I were struggling we struggled together, she and I. Now it was like I felt betrayed by my closest friend. It all seemed so unfair. After years of being an only child, I found out I had a few siblings and a brother who I knew personally from school. I never told anyone at the time. I kept right on as if it were all a bad dream that would be over when I woke up. This affected my relationship with my mother tremendously. We always still communicated but our relationship suffered for years. My father, who I thought was bringing the family down with all of his drinking, was actually not such a bad guy anymore. I realized that he never had to be there for me at all. I was very hurt and I carried much of that pain around on my shoulders for years. I tried to keep smiling at everyone but I was hurting badly.

At this time I was bagging groceries at one of the local grocery stores. After school I worked there from 4p.m. in the evening until 10 p.m. On the weekends, I usually worked from 8a.m. until 4p.m. Working these types of hours, coupled with everything else I did on the side, didn't leave much time to have a social life. One day my manager at the store pulled me to the side to give me a speech that I still remember vividly. He told me that I needed to enjoy my senior year and that I would never be able to recreate those times again. He was absolutely right, because   although I don't remember exactly what I did at work everyday back then, I do recall the many parties, and events that I missed that year while I was working. Ironically, my peers voted me "Mr. Bright Smile",for my high school class and "Mr. Sunshine" for the summit program. This made me extremely happy because with all of the things that were going on in my life, people still remembered me always smiling.

In my neighborhood, all of the young guys that I thought were successful were usually in the service. They would come back home with nice cars, and at the time, that was all I knew success to be. Immediately following my senior year I joined the United States Air Force. This also was a tremendous experience for me. This was my first time flying on an airplane. I was ready for the challenge. I started in basic training in San Antonio TX. It was the beginning of a four-year military career that was going to teach me lots of things. While in basic training I met SSgt. Jefferson who was my Training Instructor. He was a young , strong black man who I looked up to from the moment that I met him. Of course at this time he was yelling and screaming at me as he did to everyone in my flight, but still I respected the fact that he represented exactly what I thought I wanted to be at the time. This was also my first time meeting people from other cities across the United States. I met people from Detroit, New York, Chicago, Los Angeles, Virginia, Atlanta, Miami, Houston, Oakland, New Orleans and many other places as well. I was very curious about what life was like in these places. Ironically, due to the popularity of Port Arthur rap music, all of these guys wanted to know what life was like in my hometown. I figured out that most of these guys had very similar situations as me growing up. Mostly all were from broken homes and all grew up poor. I even met a guy who was born as a result of his mother getting raped at sixteen. When we all figured out just how much we had in common, we all bonded together as a team.

After six weeks of basic training, graduation time was upon us. The morning of graduation SSgt Jefferson asked the flight to think about what taps(these were the metal plates that the Instructors wore on the bottom of their shoes so you can hear them coming a mile away.) meant to us. We all agreed that the sounds of taps would forever make us think back about him as well as being in basic training. He continued to tell us that he gave away the taps off of his boots to the two most outstanding airmen in the flight. Out of approximately 50 airmen, I was one of the two recipients of a tap. This meant the world to me and to this day I still have that tap. I was eighteen at the time and I cried like a baby as we left Lackland Air Force base that morning. This touched me because someone that I looked up to and respected so much, just happened to think very highly of me too.

I left San Antonio and immediately got shipped to Biloxi, MS for technical school. I was going to spend the next eight months here learning electronics and satellite communications. Here I met lots of good people but I also met someone who would in the future become one of the best friends/brother or partners that I could have. His name was Kevin and he was cut from a different cloth. Kevin was a natural born leader who could influence people wherever he went. He had never lived in the same place for over three years his entire life. As a result he could see life a lot different than I could. I was born and raised in the same house in the same city my entire life. He taught me a lot about different things he had learned over the years. We became really good friends.

I started saving money as soon as I joined the military. When I was living at home with my mother I always tried to save money but I could never reach 1 thousand dollars. This became a goal for me. Before you knew it I had saved about twenty-five hundred. Someone in my barracks saw my bank statement and told everybody that I was rich. People would tease me about it a lot. Even though twenty-five hundred was not a lot of money, I was successful at fulfilling my goal of saving one thousand dollars. I would watch the other airmen spend every quarter of their check and be completely broke until the next payday. They would spend all of their money on clothes, food and going out. I spent all of my time in the gym working out for free.

After nine months of technical training, I left Mississippi with a newly financed vehicle, about two thousand dollars and a healthy physique. This period of time set the foundation for what was yet to come in my life. After this period I didn't have as much time on my hands to go to the gym and work out, but because of the initial sacrifice, my metabolism grew very high and I maintained a firm body even without going to the gym. Because I had saved that amount of money, I was able to buy a car without a co-signer and start building my credit at the same time. All of these things were very important for my future growth. It was a blessing that I was able to start this building process at the age of 19, but the best was still yet to come.

After leaving Biloxi, Mississippi in 1994 I went straight to my permanent duty station, which was back in San Antonio, TX where I happened to go for basic training. There I was put into an Engineering Installation Unit. This was a unit that would travel around the world to install and remove ground radio equipment. I was very pleased with the new challenge. I would get inside of my car and ride around for hours looking at all of the huge buildings and businesses and wonder about all of the opportunity in the big city. My small town didn't have a real downtown or tourist attractions so this was quite amazing to me. Staying true to my relentless pursuit of progress, I immediately started working on my degree in electronics by passing a CLEP(college level equivalency Program) two days after I got to the base. Shortly thereafter I passed another test to earn 3 more college credits. During this time, similar to the times in Biloxi, MISS, I tried to get friends to do the same thing that I was doing. And just like before, no one else was quite as excited about these things like I was.

Another thing on my to do list was to go back and speak with Sgt. Jefferson. I pulled on the side of him as he was marching his flight and spoke with him. He invited me to park and come to talk with him for a while. When we went back to his office he started digging through some pictures in his desk to reveal a picture of him and myself a year prior when I was in his basic training flight. He told me that he always kept pictures of his favorite airmen. After about a one-hour conversation, he made mention that we could hang out now and he gave me his contact information. I never contacted him again, because I wanted to remember him in the same light as I had a year ago. He represented something that up until that point didn't exist in my life. He was a young, strong, black man and that was exactly the way I wanted to remember him. I haven't seen or heard from SSgt. Jefferson since that day but I will never forget him.

I was presented an opportunity to travel to Alaska for three weeks. I was very eager to go. When we landed in Anchorage, Alaska the entire city was covered in six inches of snow. This was my first time seeing real snow so I played in it like a kid. The other ten people who went with me had grown up around snow and weren't nearly as excited to see it as I was. We stayed there for a couple of days and then headed west down the Aluetian island chain to an island called Shemia. This island was tiny. It measured two miles wide and four miles long. This little island had no trees and a little blue fox called "scruffies" were the only animals that we saw on the island. There was a bowling alley on the island with four lanes. At night, everyone on base hung out at the one little club on base. The main event in this little club was the arm-wrestling table. The people there, all had money because there was nothing there to spend it on. Everyone on my team came to the club with me on our second night on the island. There was a huge commotion as we walked in the club almost as if there was a fight happening. We found that all the racket was the result of everyone gathered around the arm-wrestling table placing their bets. When we walked in, I was picked out of the crowd to arm-wrestle a guy who had beaten all of his competitors. I beat the guy and the people on this little island treated me like a king for the next couple of weeks.

About a year and a half after moving back to San Antonio I got married to my high school sweetheart, Rolanda, who was at the time pregnant with our daughter Sydney. I drove home, to Port Arthur and got married in a small ceremony at my church. My friend Ray, let me borrow a white suit to get married in. The wedding was really wonderful. Afterwards, she packed up and moved back to San Antonio with me. I was ready for us to start our new lives together. I sold the speakers out of my car and used the money to buy us a nice little loft apartment. I was absolutely determined to make life better for my family. I vowed to myself that I would do whatever it took so that my family could enjoy a happy life. Two months after we were married at the age of twenty I got qualified for our first new house. It was a small brick home with a one-car garage. It took about four months to build.

On October 8th 1995, my life took another drastic turn with the birth of my beautiful daughter, Sydney. As I held her tiny body in my arms, I vowed to myself that I would make her life better than mine. I thought about how much she depended on me for everything. This drove me even harder.

I was now a 21-year-old husband, father, and a homeowner. I took a part time job as a security guard at a car dealership to help pay the bills. This was perfect because it allowed me to make money while studying for college. I would sit at work and think about what I could do to make more money to ease the family's financial load. Due to the efforts put in place at my military job, I was awarded Airman Of the Quarter for the communications squadron, Kelly Air Force Base, and the San Antonio Air Logistics Center. This was quite an accomplishment for a young airman.

Around this same time I met the owner of an insurance agency who told me I would be a great insurance salesman. He paid for me to go to a class to prepare for the insurance exam. I was fortunate enough to receive my Associate Of Applied Science degree in Electronic Systems Technology on the same day that I passed the State insurance exam. Immediately after, I began to sell life insurance policies to military personnel every evening. This was my first time starting to see extra money at the end of the month. I was good at the selling but I enjoyed it because I never sold anyone anything that they could not afford or that they didn't need. There was a manager in the office, who told me that it was not my call to determine what people could or couldn't afford and he urged me to try to sell everything we had every time I went out. His philosophy on selling wasn't one that I could agree with so I quit the job while maintaining my integrity.

Immediately following this I met a friend by the name of Troy who introduced me to network marketing. We were selling telephone services for a while until his enlistment was up. He moved to Austin Texas to open up a barbeque restaurant, while I stayed in San Antonio. This network marketing business was something that fit my character but I could never duplicate my efforts when speaking to my peers about the business. My friends at this point were not really thinking about business. Individuals who were older than me didn't want to get involved with the business because they felt that they had seen it all or heard it all before, so what could a 21 year old teach them about making money. This was somewhat discouraging but I kept on looking forward. During these times of my life I remember wishing that I could win a small lottery for like ten thousand dollars to help ease the family's financial burdon. People would often tell me that I was crazy for wanting to win ten thousand instead of ten million. My response was that I knew one day I would make it and I wanted to be able to say that I did it myself.

Time was now winding down on my four-year military commitment and I felt like I was ready for the world. I was offered a job at another insurance company, as well as a position in Austin Texas at a Semiconductor equipment manufacturing company called Applied Materials Inc.

I took the job in Austin and set out for a new career as a final test technician. I began to rent the house that I had purchased in San Antonio and received a small monthly profit. My family and I moved next door to my friend Troy and his family who were living in a quadro-plex that was in a pretty rough neighborhood. Troy now had quit the restaurant business and was starting at the ground floor of a now successful telecommunications company. Back in the neighborhood, we were again surrounded by despair and negativity. I had just moved my family from a nice neighborhood where my daughter could run freely down the side-walks. In the months that I lived in this place, I witness a few fist fights, arson , and a couple of shootings. One day someone fatally shot the neighborhood ice cream man.

By this time I was 22 years old working for a fortune 500 company and already had rental property. The first three months that I worked for the company I rarely ever took a lunch break. There was so much to learn and so little time to take it all in that I figured it would be best for me to take my training into my own hands. I hated the times when we would have meetings and management would speak about training the new people. I hated that feeling of being the new guy. I had just left an arena where I was one of the most knowledgeable workers and now I was starting over again. Fortunately the new guy syndrome didn't last very long. I took a night shift position to assist my wife in taking care of our daughter while she finished Nursing school. Little did I know then that I was going to meet another set of life long friends on night shift. Particularly one friend by the name of Kerby who was someone I identified with very well. He had been trading stocks for a couple of years and as our friendship grew he taught me everything he knew about the stock market. Before I knew it, I had an internet stock account and was trading stocks and options on a regular basis. The same kid who 12 months ago was wishing to win a ten thousand dollar lottery now was trading an average of thirty thousand dollars. Crazy as it may sound I really still thought I was broke based on the fact that my partner had so much more money than I had.

I got picked to go on a trip to Taiwan to install a piece of equipment. This was my first time leaving the United States. I was installing the semi-conductor equipment in a wafer processing fab in a part of Taiwan that was still very primitive. There was a rice field outside of the company and also a few goats would often be lingering around the entrance. As I watched how those people lived, it made me think about the conditions that I grew up. This place had open sewers, so there was always a really bad smell in the air. I had never experienced anything like this in my life, so how is it that these people could have positive attitudes while smelling sewage all day long? I was on the other side of the world, literally by myself. I had to take a 45-minute cab ride to and from work with a cab driver that I couldn't even speak with. As I would ride home with the cab driver at night, we had to pass through the mountainous countryside, where I made it a point to pray to God. I made the best out of the trip and gave the project my two hundred percent. The project was a success but while I was gone the company had a layoff. As I sat down watching the news announcing the reduction in force I became very worried. I knew I couldn't continue to live my life worried about lay offs. I knew how to make money in the stock market but in order to make enough money to live, I knew I had to have quite a bit of money that I won't be able to save up if I get laid off. Soon after I made it back to Austin a job opening came up in Dallas, Texas. This was perfect because my good friend Kerby was retiring from the company to pursue full time stock trading. Once again I was losing someone that I had grown very close to.

Before the move, my wife and I began driving up to Dallas on the weekends to search for real estate. I found a house that was almost done being built in a brand new community just outside of Dallas, TX. They called this a Spec home and since it wasn't originally being built to my exact specifications, the builder knocked twenty two thousand off of the price. Since I had already found somewhere to live, I took the relocation money that the company would have used to house me for two months and used that money as a down payment on the house. Even though I had plenty of funds to pay as a down payment I was able to creatively come up with a way for the company to pay for it. Things were going really well at the job and

I was even fortunate enough to be Employee of the Quarter. Things were really going well at this point in my life.

My friend Kevin who I had met years back in Biloxi, Miss had moved up to Dallas to work for the same company that I was working. He was excited to be in a new city again and we had a chance to think of how we could take the next step to change our family's financial destiny.

The job now had me traveling quite a bit. I enjoyed traveling because I would get a chance to meet so many new people. I particularly enjoyed the people I would meet on the airplane. I would always strike up conversations with the other passengers to find out their line of work. I learned a little bit about various occupations and small businesses. Thinking ahead of myself, as usual, I bought my first Rolex watch so I could have something of value to pass down to my kids. When I wore it on the airplane, lots of executives and business owners would see it and strike up conversations with me. When they found that I was knowledgeable of real estate, and stock options, they would continue to talk to me and teach me more about other subjects. They would talk about life in general and speak of how their parents expected them to be successful. They often knew their ancestor's occupations dating back to the 1800's. They would also tell me of great inheritances that they received from parents, aunts and uncles. They told me that their parents prepared them financially for life, similar to the way my uncles had taught me to play ping pong. It was strange because they mostly felt that their success or status was a direct result of their up bringing which is why they went to such lengths to make sure their kids went to the best schools. Some found me interesting because they couldn't figure out how my up bringing could bring me to a place were I could converse on their level about certain topics. The most consistent thing that I heard from all of these gentlemen was that real estate was the way to go to build wealth.

When the company traveling came to an end I had accumulated quite a bit of money. I decided to invest it into real estate as I was instructed. I was calling ads in the newspaper about houses, duplexes, and four-plexes for sale. After reading all of the books and purchasing all of the kits that I would see on the television pertaining to real estate, I was finally able to get my feet wet and start buying investment properties. I invested in a nice real estate portfolio and once again was on my way with little experience.

On May 11th 2001, my life was once again changed forever with the birth of my son, Marcus Jr. I now had one more reason to work hard for my family.

The tragic events of September 11, 2001 are events that will never erase from my memory. The entire country was devastated and none of our lives would ever quite be the same. My wife and I went from celebrating the baby's four-month birthday to wondering what was going to happen next. This was by far the most significant event in history that had happened in my lifetime. Thousands of lives lost and the security of the entire country seemed to be threatened.

Myself, like ever other American, took a great financial lost after this. I lost my small fortune in the stock market and my once profitable real estate venture was now facing ten thousand dollar per month loss. I was absolutely devastated and things continued to get worse. I was still working full time and the money I made from my job couldn't cover the losses that I was taking. Once again I was in a situation involving the lack of money. There was no one I could go to and ask for ten thousand dollars per month to keep me going so I kept my issues to myself. Of course, I didn't sleep at night and I was very stressed. At some times it was even hard to eat. All my life I had planned to always have finances so I could never be in the same position as we were when I was a child. Now I was faced with a situation that I couldn't have planned. I truly felt like I was being tested. I was right back in the position that I worked all my life so diligently to get out. I began working harder and staying up later and later at night trying to figure out a way to fix this mess. No matter what I did, at this point I couldn't physically dig my way out of this one. I was sinking into a deep depression and could barely focus at home or at work.

A good friend of mine gave me a book called <u>Adversity Creates Opportunity</u>. It was written by a gentleman named Eric Farrington. I read the book and found it interesting. Eric had worked in real estate for about twenty years.

This gentlemen had been through a lot and was still keeping a positive attitude. Shortly after reading the book, myself and my friend Kevin, had the opportunity to meet Mr. Farrington. As we met him for the first time we immediately figured out that he was someone we needed to spend more time around. He believed that God had put us together for a reason and he took to myself and Kevin almost like sons. He taught us how to actually use that faith that I heard preached about all my life. He taught me to slow down and not to worry because God has already fixed your problems. With all of the efforts I put forth, I had made little progress at trying to turn around my situation. The moment that I let go and let God, all of those situations worked themselves out, one by one. I was able to resolve my losses in my first real estate venture and started over with a ton of experience.

Kevin and I invested in a partnership with Eric and things began to turn around. Now walking by faith and not by sight, opportunities just continued to come our way. We continued to work, pray and persevere together and less than a year from the horrible tragedy that rocked the entire nation, I was able to walk away from a six-figure income, financially independent, with a completely new attitude on life. I had everything in life that I thought was important. I had a big house with fine cars, clothes and jewelry. None of these things could ever compare to the peace you have in your life when you truly place your faith in God. I pray that something in my story will enable you to overcome whatever it is that you may be going through.

I spoke about my childhood in a gloomy tone to prove a point. We all have problems in our lives that can affect us in many different ways. Remember that the key is to always stay positive. There is a positive side to whatever it is you have been through or currently going through.

So now, when asked the question from the front of the book "Do you feel you are a product of your surroundings?" I gladly reply; "Yes, I am." My surroundings were actually very positive;

-I am the product of a mother who loved me unconditionally. A mother who told me that I could accomplish whatever I want to accomplish in life. A mother who loved me enough to never let me get out of line. A mother who kept me in church. I love you mama.

-The product of a father who stuck by me no matter what. A father who would sit up at night and eat egg and rice with me. A father who was proud to call me his son. Richard, you have always been a wonderful father. I love you daddy.

-The product of having had the pleasure of knowing all four of my grandparents.

-The product of a grandmother who prepared the best tasting food I've ever eaten my life. A grandmother who always made me feel special. I love you Big Mama.

-The product of grandfather who was so proud of me in his older age that it made me nervous. I wish we would have had more time to spend together. I love you Mitch(Rest in Peace). I dedicated this entire book to your memory.

-The product of a grandmother who taught me to "let my little light shine." I'm trying my best grandma. I love you.

-The product of a grandfather who was my first role model. The kind of man that all young men should strive to be like. I love you grandpa.

-The product of many cousins, aunts and uncles who have always supported me. It's too many of ya'll to name. I love you all.

- The product of a community that would help to keep all the kids in line.

-The product of a next-door- neighbor who treated me like her own son. A neighbor who cooked for me and would go out of her way for anyone. I love you Mrs. Gill.

-The product of a wonderful wife who stood by me, despite the fact that her husband is a dreamer. A wife who has always been a wonderful mother to my two kids. I love you Rolanda.

-The product of growing up in a community where we could play down the street and around the corner, and everyone went home safely when it got dark.

-The product of a church home that treated me like family. I love you Mt. Sinai.

-The product of a pastor who would always say "work now while it is day, for night is coming when no man can work"

-The product of a high school that gave me, and all of the kids in the community something to be proud of. We all looked forward to the day we could say we were Lincoln High School Bumblebees like most of our parents.

-The product of close friends who treated me like a brother.

-The product of teachers and principals who pushed me to be the best.

-The product being raised around many good people with big hearts.

-The product of a city where everybody spoke to each other.

- The product of many friends of different races who taught me lots of different things about life.

-The product of classmates and friends who always helped to keep me out of trouble.

-The product of a big family who always protected me.

-The product of having fathered the two most wonderful children on earth.

-The product of God's ultimate plan for my life.

Remember, that no matter what you are going through, there is a light at the end of the tunnel. Keep your focus on the positive side of things, never the negative side. Allow your adversity to fuel your drive to succeed at whatever you want to do in life. Lastly, remember to keep your faith in God. He holds the ultimate plan.

"It is impossible to please God without faith"
Hebrews 11:6

"People might not get all they work for in this world, but they must certainly work for all they get."
Frederick Douglas

Relentless

Relentless
Is the word I choose,
To describe a person
Who has seen the blues.

But they never give up
Though hard it may seem,
Just stay focused on your goals
You'll fulfill your dreams.

It describes the single mother
With no where to go,
Who makes a way for her children
Allowing them to grow.

It describes the adult
Raised with no direction,
But still gives others
Lots of love and affection.

It describes the young boy
With a terminal disease,
Who gives a positive word
To everyone he sees.

Marcus A. Parker

It describes the father
Who just lost his job,
But finds a quick gig
To help feed his kid.

Life will always be filled with
Adversity and pain,
Stay relentless
And you'll find sunshine after the rain.

Marcus A. Parker

"Character is what you know you are, not what others think you have."
Marva Collins

Self Worth

I always had a very low sense of self- worth. I knew my family's situation and realized that there was no room to pay for any typical kid nonsense. I was always treated as an adult because of my demeanor. I can recall a time when I was around nine or ten I went to spend a couple of weeks with my great grandparents in Louisiana. My grandmother had to run errands with a friend for a couple of hours but my great-grandmother needed constant supervision. My Grandmother went on to tell her friend that I would stay and watch the house and that I wasn't like the other kids. She felt that I could be trusted like an adult. When they left, I watched the other kids my age and older play in a distant field. I wondered to myself if my behavior was really such a good thing. While the other kids played I was stuck being a grown up. This scenario would haunt me on into every facet of my adult life. My biggest strength would also prove to be my biggest weakness. At work, and in relationships, I always succeeded in suppressing my own desires in order to please someone else. No one ever stopped to tell me that what I wanted was very important too. I had identified people who wanted their desires met as being selfish. It took some time for me to realize that we need to let our desires be known and met. In friendships as well as relationships we should focus on showing ourselves to others instead of selling ourselves. In other words show people who you really are and let them accept you or reject you but at least they are accepting or rejecting the real you. In school I was always one of the class clowns. I later figured out that the main reason was because I needed to feel like I was doing the entertaining. I never felt worthy of being entertained by someone else. Always remember that you are important because God loves you. There is something unique about all of us. If you have not found that "something" just yet, don't give up, it's just not your time yet. By this point in the book, you may have realized that my life was not all peaches and cream. Whether you have experienced more or less adversity than I did really doesn't matter. The sky is the limit for you, and if you can believe in yourself, there is no limit to what you can accomplish. What I am trying to say is that you should always love yourself and remember that you are someone special.

Marcus A. Parker

"You can't hold a man down without staying down with him."
Booker T. Washington

Goal Setting

Success in anything requires the ability to set goals and always follow through with your plans. This is a key that most people never figure out. Whatever you do, you must keep in mind why you are doing it, and what step this action is taking toward your goal. As an example; I have seen many people go to college with a goal of getting a degree in a certain field. A year into the program the student decides to buy a vehicle to have transportation to the part time job. Then the situation or time gets so hectic that the student quits school to have more time for the part time job. This is a very typical situation. The student completely lost focus of the original goal of completing the college degree. Once we get into the habit of setting goals we have to follow through, stay focused , and not let distractions get us off track. Your goals do not have to be far fetched. You can set very modest, attainable, short-term goals for yourself. I recommend that you start right away with something as simple as going the entire weekend and only spending 10 dollars. I became extremely addicted to goal setting and began enjoying the struggle of reaching the goal just as much as achieving the actual goal.

The first thing you should do is establish what your goals are. Secondly, write them down and keep them in a place where you can see them. Thirdly, you should write down the steps necessary to accomplish this goal. Lastly, follow through with those steps and watch your dreams become reality.

"There are no secrets to success. It is the result of preparation, hard work, and learning from failure."
Colin Powell

Following Through

Growing up, I heard many people speak about what they wanted and what they were going to do. Sadly enough, I learned the hard way that most of the time it was only talk. As I grew older and would follow through with the goals I spoke about, people started to see it in me and respected the fact that I would conquer the goals I set out to achieve. Following through is a very important step in reaching your goals. It is the initial step that starts the engine. We can easily write down goals but it won't get us anywhere until we follow through with an action plan to make those goals reality. If you've ever stepped on to an elevator, you knew that you wanted to go to a certain floor in the building. That is like setting a goal. Following through is actually pressing the button for the floor you want to go to. Even though you got on the elevator, you were not going to go anywhere without following through and pressing the button.

Marcus A. Parker

This is exactly how we must follow through with the goals we set. Always try your best to complete whatever task you start. I recommend starting out every morning with a "to do" list. This will start you on your way and will also give you a sense of accomplishment at the end of the day. Completing your daily tasks will automatically make you feel successful, which is exactly what you are.

"The ultimate measure of a man is not where he stands in moments of comfort, but where he stands at times of challenge and controversy."
Rev. Dr. Martin Luther King Jr.

Time Management

Time management is another very important aspect of success in life. Time does not stop or slow down for any of us but it can be used to your advantage by savoring every minute. When I was in the Air Force I worked a part time job as a security guard at a car lot. Most of the other employees would bring a small television or a radio to work with them to help kill time. I used this time to study for college level equivalence tests also known as (CLEP) tests. I completed six college courses while working as a security guard part time for approximately four months. I was also blessed to have received an Associate of Applied Science in Electronics Systems Technology on the same day that I received a group 1 life and health insurance license. All of these things taught me a lot, and I was able to use them all later in life. Time is like a deadly weapon; it can be your best friend or your worst enemy, depending on how it is used. Always try to use your time wisely. Make it a priority to not waste time. One way to help leverage your time properly is to do things in parallel. Imagine how long it would take to finish cooking dinner if you only cooked one entrée at a time. Usually when we cook, everything that is going to be cooked is usually started in parallel. Keep this in mind in everything that you do. Remember, none of us know exactly how much time we have on this Earth, so be sure and make every moment count for something.

"One man with courage makes a majority"
Andrew Jackson

True Education

Lots of people think that education is only achieved in a school or University. The word education means to provide with knowledge or training. This can be achieved by reading books or listening to individuals who are experienced in certain areas. I truly believe that we have something to learn from everyone. Don't get me wrong, I am an advocate of college education and wish everyone could attend an institution of higher learning at some point in their lifetime. The thing that I am against is the idea that you need college or specialized training in order to excel in certain areas. Never limit yourself based on what the world says you are capable of doing. In other words never determine ones worth or usefulness based on his or her's label i.e. college degrees/job titles/etc. Experience will always reign supreme over textbook education. Always allow your mind to open up. A person once said " the mind is like a

Marcus A. Parker

parachute, it works best when it is open." There are lessons in life to be learned every single day. Even if that lesson is what " NOT" to do, you can still learn from that. Set a goal to learn something every day. You will notice a huge change in your overall outlook. Remember, "The more you know, the more you grow" . The more things that you have knowledge of, will allow you to have conversations or things to talk about with more people. This in return will give you more people to learn from. It is like a chain reaction. Pretty soon, you find that you can match wit with virtually anyone who is not ignorant. We all know that ignorance is the lack of knowledge. We are all ignorant about something. The difference is that I consider an ignorant person someone who doesn't know anything because they think they know everything. Always stay humble and listen to everything people have to say to you. Then you make the decision whether or not you agree with what they say. Always strive to educate yourself in whatever way possible. Please remember one of my personal quotes; "Ignorance is Optional".

"If there is no struggle,
there is no progress"
Frederick Douglas

Battling Negativity

I personally consider negativity to be a deadly drug. Once you allow negativity into your life, it can have a tremendous affect on your personal progress. Try your best to look at the positive side of everything. If it is a very rainy day, think about how good this is for the plants and the grass instead of complaining because the sun is not shining. When your overall attitude is positive, you will notice yourself growing further away from people who think or talk very negatively. Personally, I have never done anything without having someone say something negative to me about whatever I was doing. Fortunately, I learned early on that this is a common thing. Lots of times people can be negative around you and mean you absolutely no harm. To prevent this, I recommend keeping your goals to yourself so they are not subject to someone's opinion that may kill your dream. I urge you to go an entire week and only speak positively. Soon this will become a part of your overall character. Most of the things in life that we speak negatively about can't be changed by us anyway. Don't worry about things that you can't fix. Keep thinking positively and focus on your goals and the things that you can fix. Negativity, depression and worry can not only hinder your progress, but can also lead to health issues such as high blood pressure. Once you eliminate your negative thinking you will find that all of your problems will eventually pass anyway, so why stress over anything. Once I got a speeding ticket when I was in the Air Force. Some sort of way the paperwork got mixed up and my letter didn't make it to the judge in the small town that I was speeding through. I was sent out of town for two months with my military job, so I had no correspondence about this ticket. When I returned to San Antonio, Texas I had a class for working as a back-up Security policeman. While in the class my instructor ran my driver's license after I told him what had happened a few months back. A warrant had already been issued for me because of the ticket. Since I was able to explain my story I wasn't taken to jail, but a state trooper came picked me up and brought me to an ATM machine to take out my

240 dollar balance. At the time I was twenty-one years old, with a new born child, a wife, a mortgage and two car payments. That 240 dollars took my net worth down to around 0. I was so stressed that I had to be taken to the hospital that day and given muscle relaxers to ease my tension. All of the muscles in my neck and back had tightened at the same time and I could barely move my head. All of this stress lead to physical problems with my body. This is because, at the time, all I could see were all of my many responsibilities but no money. Had I been walking by faith and not by sight, I probably could have stayed away from the hospital that day. Little did I know that just a few years down the road I'd be financially independent. God loves us and has already worked out the things that we are stressing about so the key is to never live stressed.

In my lifetime, people have stolen from me, cheated me, and lied to me. You must keep in mind that the human factor will always leave room for these types of circumstances. When things like this happen, remember that there is still a positive side. God is teaching you a lesson, so try your best to pay attention and learn from it.

"Both tears and sweat are salty, but they render a different result. Tears will get you sympathy; sweat will get you change."
Rev. Jesse Jackson

A word from the Author

At age 27 I stopped and evaluated my life. My family and I were living in our third new house in a resort-styled community, equipped with golf course, water-park and stocked fish-ponds. I was actually living better than most of the people I had watched on television as a kid. My wife and children had the best of everything. All of this and I had just quit a six-figure career. I was basicly retired.

Upon further reflection, I found that I was still very unhappy. I had not yet begun to live my life. All I had done was worked. Running from the statistics surrounding the life of a young black male, I was just as enslaved as the individuals who were locked away in prison. I had become just as addicted to progress as the drug addicts were addicted to crack. While I was basicly the "poster boy" for those who would say "you don't have to be a product of your environment", I truly was a product of mine. I spent so much time thinking of how to break the financial curse that had afflicted my family that I rarely could sleep the entire night. I couldn't sit down to watch a sports event because I felt like I was wasting time that I didn't have.

When I learned to truly utilize my faith in God my entire life took a huge turn for the better. No longer did I have to spend every moment thinking of what I need to do to fix things because I learned that God had already fixed all of the things that I would find myself worrying about. I included the Serenity Prayer in the book to share with you, and hopefully it can bless you as much as it has blessed me.

Many black mothers, throughout the years have asked me to talk with their sons, nephews, etc. in order for them to try to be like me. I would often answer that I never wanted anyone to try and be like me. I want them to be much better than me. I want them to realize that your dreams can become a reality. I want them to realize that poverty, as we knew it, was never about the lack of funds but the lack of information. I want everyone to realize that whatever struggle you are going through is just God's way of teaching you something.

I realize that the life of intercity black youths is very misunderstood. I published this book with my own funds so that I wouldn't have to edit what I feel God has placed on my heart to say to all of my people who are dealing with any type of adversity. I wanted this book to be easy to read and to be uplifting to you. I also would like to encourage all black youth to read. Reading opens up so many doors. As you read in my story, I got lots of training in life by meeting people who had something to share with me. Reading allows you to have the same experiences without having to travel the world.

Over the years I had become one of the hardest working people you ever want to meet. The word work-a-holic was such an understatement in describing my life. I had taken in so much information over the past ten years that it was even hard for me to complete a statement without jumping subjects. My mind was so loaded with information that I couldn't even sit still. Hard work brought me a certain level of material wealth. This in turn made life difficult because when others would see my material status they would treat me as if I were special. We are all God's children and are special in his eyes. True wealth is inside of you, not in your bank account. Remember, only judge individuals by their character, never financial status.

I will continue to pray for you and I ask you to continue to pray for me and my family. My next goal is to read the entire Bible in a year. I wish you the absolute best at accomplishing whatever goals you have in life.

God Bless

"The burden of being black is that you have to be superior just to be equal. But the glory of it is that once you achieve, you have achieved indeed."

Jesse Jackson

Final Thanks

Again I would like to thank God for his many blessings and allowing me to complete this book.

I would like to thank all of the people in my life who have helped me learn so much. To my mother, thanks for always keeping me in line over the years. I would like to thank my father for his support. I would like to thank the Parker family and the Mitchell family for all of their support. I would also like to thank the Polk family. I would like to thank the Port Arthur Independent School District, including all of my coaches and teachers who believed in me and supported me throughout the years. I would like to send a special thanks to the memory of Abraham Lincoln High School, particularly the class of 1993. I used the purple and gold colors on the cover as a tribute to my high school and all of those who share that bumblebee pride. I would like to thank PHS(Program for Human

Services). I fully support programs like these that help young kids see things in life. Thanks for everything. I would like to send a special thanks to everyone in the City of Port Arthur's personnel department. Thank you all for your support over the years, and for treating me like family. I would like to thank everyone at Mt. Sinai Missionary Baptist Church for always believing in me. Thanks to all of my close friends and associates in the United States Air Force. I would like to thank all of my friends in Austin, Tx, particularly my family from final test. You all continue to make it happen. I would like to say thanks to all of my friends in Dallas, Tx. To anyone I may have left out, I want to say thanks to you as well.

"Think like a queen. A queen is not afraid to fail. Failure is another steppingstone to greatness."
Oprah Winfrey

"If you don't stand for something you will fall for anything."
Malcolm X

"We have something to learn from everyone; Even if the lesson is what Not to do."
Marcus A. Parker

"Ignorance is Optional."
Marcus A. Parker

"Pain is the best fuel to drive progress."
Marcus A. Parker

Marcus A. Parker

I would love to hear any of your Positive feedback.

My address is:

3523   McKinney   Ave #539
Dallas, Tx 75204-1401

Thanks,
Marcus A. Parker
Or visit me on the web at
www.marcusaparker.com

The Serenity Prayer

God grant me the serenity to accept the things I cannot change; The courage to change the things I can and the wisdom to know the difference.

Amen

Printed in the United States
38983LVS00001B/59